# Needle Felting for Beginners

The Complete Step by Step User Guide to Craft Out Awesome Needle Felting Projects and Lifelike Needle Felted Animals and More with Wool

By

Alice Green

## Disclaimer

This publication is designed to provide competent and reliable information regarding the subject matter covered. However, the views expressed in this publication are those of the author alone, and should not be taken as expert instruction or professional advice. The reader is responsible for his or her own actions.

The author hereby disclaims any responsibility or liability whatsoever that is incurred from the use or application of the contents of this publication by the purchaser or reader. The purchaser or reader is hereby responsible for his or her own actions.

# Books By The Same Author

*Modern Macramé Book for Beginners and Beyond*

*Cricut for Beginners*

# Table of Contents


Books By The Same Author .................................................... 3

Introduction ......................................................................... 7

Chapter 1 ............................................................................ 11

What is Needle Felting? ..................................................... 11

    Background History of Needle Felting ........................... 12

    How Does Needle Felting Work? .................................. 15

    Therapeutic Benefits of Needle Felting ......................... 18

Chapter 2 ............................................................................ 22

Basic Needle Felting Terminologies .................................. 22

Chapter 3 ............................................................................ 28

Top Needle Felting Tips and Tricks .................................. 28

Chapter 4 ............................................................................ 36

Getting Started With Needle Felting ................................ 36

    Basic Tools and Materials Needed ................................ 36

        Wool roving ............................................................. 36

Felting needle ............................................................. 37

Scissors ..................................................................... 41

Felting Pad ................................................................ 42

Additional Tools and Materials (Optional) ...................... 47

Needle holders ........................................................... 48

Carding brushes ......................................................... 49

Formers .................................................................... 50

Chapter 5 ..................................................................... 51

Crafting Needle Felting Projects ..................................... 51

Felted Strawberries ...................................................... 51

Felted Dog ................................................................ 55

Felted Buttons ........................................................... 62

Felted Owls ............................................................... 64

Felted Cats ................................................................ 68

Felted Mouse ............................................................. 72

Mini Decorative Pillow ................................................ 76

Felt Fat Plants ............................................................ 78

Felt Ball Earrings ........................................................ 83

Felt Pin-Cushion ........................................................ 85

Felt Corsage ............................................................... 88

Felt Coasters ........................................................... 90

Felt Eye Mask ......................................................... 92

Monogram Felt Pouch ............................................ 97

Felt Christmas Tree ............................................... 100

Chapter 6 ............................................................... 106

Needle Felting Frequently Asked Questions (FAQs) ......... 106

Conclusion .............................................................. 111

# Introduction

Everyone, to an extent, appreciates art.

This could be arguable, but it explains why you can decide to sit down for a relaxing afternoon after a week full of work, and what you are settling down to do will be to reproduce the beautiful knit work you saw somewhere online. For some reason, you could not tell, you were drawn to the intricacies of the design, and although you could not quite make sense of all that you had seen, it did not change the fact that you were going to replicate that design to the best of your abilities.

So, Saturday evening meets you on the reclining chair, working on the design you saved for the weekend while the voice of your favorite classical musicians fills the evening air. It is a challenging project - no doubt - but you would be lying if you tried to deny the fact that there is something about the project that thrills you to your bone marrows.

The love for art.

That's exactly what takes you to the art gallery's commissioning taking place down the street you live in. You probably do not understand most of what you will see in the art gallery and some of the art pieces that would be on display may just look like a bunch of crap to you. However, there are those that you would love, and that would cause you to stand before them for long minutes, staring at them in wonder and marveling at the craftmanship displayed by the artist who created them. In those few minutes, you would not be able to deny the fact that a good art piece, no matter how abstract it may seem to you, always seems to be able to draw you in and grab your attention.

There are probably a thousand different scenarios to explain this. Everyone loves art to some extent. Even if you do not quite agree to this, there may just be a little part of you that tries to rebel occasionally by reaching out to the beauty of art.

That's even the better thing about it. Art can be appreciated on different levels by different people. For some, they believe that they need to be actively involved in the creation process. These people, like the painters, writers, singers, etc. love to be the ones who make the magic happen. On the other hand, others are content with standing on the sidelines and watching things unfold. They are the ones that prefer to go to see the complete works of art, and appreciate them as best as they can. That's the great thing about art; there's something in it for everyone.

As a lover of art, you have probably heard about felting and how the process can be adapted to create phenomenal art projects. This book is directed toward; helping you harness your felting skills and getting you to the point where you can create beautiful artworks and advanced crafts all by yourself.

First off, felting is the process of making use of felt (which is a textile material) to create amazing craftworks and pieces of art. Needle felting is a kind of felting carried out with the aid of a specific kind of needle. If you have been looking for a new kind of art to explore or thinking of ways to get creative around the house and get some things done (as you would see in later sections of this book), you may want to consider going into needle felting.

And there is nothing to be scared about.

This book contains just enough information to get you started with needle felting, even if you are just a beginner. Within the pages that follow, you will learn all the basics of needle felting, why you should consider felting as a regular part of your life, felting tips and tricks you can apply to improve your skills, and everything you can think of that concerns needle felting.

There are crash courses for almost anything. Think of this book as a crash book/guide to needle felting. By the time you are done, you should be able to create some phenomenal felting projects and execute on the ideas in your head.

If you are ready, then let's get started

# Chapter 1

## What is Needle Felting?

Needle felting is an intricate process that uses barbed needles to interlock wool fibers to form a strong and condensed material. Simply put, needle felting is the process of sculpting felt (a special kind of wool) into something better and more beautiful than the original state of the felt. Normally, wool fibers have a property that makes them suitable for this purpose. Wool fibers, when rubbed together, latch onto themselves and hold on together. This forms a denser material known as felt.

Felt, on the other hand, is a textile material that is produced by matting, condensing and pressing fibers (preferably wool fibers) together. On a broader scale, felt can be made from a host of natural fibers like wool and fur or other synthetic materials like petroleum-based acrylic. Because of the special characteristics of felt, it can be used for a wide range of activities and crafts that are both creative and beneficial to the felt craft users.

## Background History of Needle Felting

Needle felting is not entirely new. As a matter of fact, the practice of felting dates as far back as 6300BC, where felt served many purposes. If you are a lover of history or you make it a point of duty to interact with content that talk of the world and how things were many centuries ago, you wouldn't be surprised to learn of this.

According to history, needle felting dates back to 6300BC. These reports show that felt is one of the oldest fabrics available to mankind. Documentations of the writing of the past refer to felt as being a major part of civilization. According to Sumerian legend, the secret of felt making was uncovered by Urnamman of Lagash.

The stories and documentation of history have it that Urnamman was a mighty and well-known warrior from Lagash. He was known for his conquests, wide travels, discoveries, and interestingly, his sense of compassion and empathy for people in his time. On the flip side, some people believe that Urnamman was not a real person but a mythical being from another realm who had been sent by the powers above to act as a judge/savior for those who needed saving. In any case, history points the discovery of felt back to this figure; mythical or not. However, for the Christians, felt and felt making was discovered by two men of high repute who were at the time, fleeing persecution; St Clement and St Christopher. Because of their need to be healthy and alive while travelling and seeking shade from the people after them, these men were forced to look for ways to make their journey as easy as it could get. The result of this was that they were able to seek out the opportunities to make use of the wool that they were able to get off the backs of dead sheep to create felt clothes and protective garment for themselves. One of the first results of this decision was the discovery that felt was an amazing material, especially for the cold weather.

After felt was first discovered, it was noted that it had quite a lot of uses that were needed in the civilization at the time. A classical example was how the men of the time were known to pack their sandals with felt. The reason for this action was that the felt seemed to provide some amount of comfort for them and prevent their feet from getting hurt as they escaped from persecution or travelled long distances. Soon enough, it was also discovered that felt was quite useful for warming the body as well.

The first concrete mention of the production of felt can be traced back to Asia. In the Altai mountains of Siberia, there was evidence that felt had been created in that place. From then, felt making and production began to get mainstream. By the end of this time frame, what had started as the men packing felt into their sandals to prevent themselves from getting hurt as they fled for their lives or travelled long distances had quickly morphed into the creation of felt stockings. This was a win-win because with the same felt, the people were able to achieve two major benefits simultaneously. They were able to answer the question of warmth (as felt is thick and the stockings could wrap around their legs and prevent coldness), and at the same time, they did not have to worry about getting blisters on their feet again.

The idea that felt could be turned into something as definite in shape and function as a pair of stockings opened up the door for something bigger.

Around 1950, the concept of needle felting started gaining grounds in the industrial setting. The first application was in the creation of industrial, building and musical instruments.

Over the years, the uses of felt have evolved as man's needs evolved and humans began to see and learn better ways of doing things. Needle felting came up due to the discovery that one of the easiest ways of matting wool together to create felt was by sticking barbed needles into the wool and pulling them out again. The idea is that the needles get into the wool and cause the material's fibers to interlock. Since wool is usually made up of distinct fibers brought together, getting them to interlock is not too much of a hard task. As the years unfold, the use of felt and how people can create great crafts out of them has been increasing. As you would see within the pages that follow, there is more to needle felting now than just stabbing needles into wool and hoping for the best. Although, that pretty much serves as the basic stage of the craft.

**How Does Needle Felting Work?**

Now that you know the origin of needle felting and how it became so popular in record time, it is vital you know exactly how this process is wired to work. This knowledge will help you as you loom to create great needle felting projects for yourself and for other purposes in the future.

This is how needle felting works;

A. Everything you will achieve with needle felting is dependent on whether or not you are skilled with making proper use of the needle. In a later part of this book, we will look at how the felting needle is and the reasons for the needle's physical structure.

B. There are tiny barbs at the bottom of every felting needle. The barbs are positioned around the sides of the needle, and there is a reason for this.

C. When you stab the needle into the material you are working with (wool material, or fur), the barbs grab the strands of wool. Remember what we pointed out earlier. If you take a close look at wool, you will see that the fibers are not as closely-knitted as other clothing materials like cotton. With your eyes, you will see the fibers of the material, and it is even possible to hold on to one fiber and pull it until the whole fabric unravels. This nature of wool is what makes it ideal for felting, among many other reasons.

D. When barbs from the felting needle hold on to the wool fibers, you are meant to pull the needle in one direction. This makes sure that the fibers that have been caught in the needle are moved in the direction of the pull, and because they do not go back in the other direction (where you pulled them from), you would have started interlocking the fibers from the fabrics you are trying to combine.

E. Stabbing the needle into the wool repeatedly will ensure that what has been spoken of in the last point happens in different parts of the fabrics. Depending on how much you were able to stab the fabrics, you will discover that you have created one continuous piece of fabric.

F. There are tiny scales on each shaft of the fibers. When fibers begin to get dragged across fabrics by your needle, they will begin to interlock. Stabbing the felting needle into the fabrics, again and again, will make them get denser, and the result is that the fabrics will begin to bunch up the more.

This is a summary of how felting by needle works. It is all about using a specified kind of needle to interlock wool fibers together until you have gotten exactly what you are looking for. With this in mind, needle felting is not a herculean task. All you need to know is how to get it done, and that is what this book is all about.

## Therapeutic Benefits of Needle Felting

Sounds unbelievable, right?

However, there is no lie in the statement above.

Needle felting has been associated with some therapeutic advantages. This is probably one of the major reasons why many people venture into it; because it is not just all about the fun of creating something new out of old materials.

These are the therapeutic benefits of needle felting

1. Felting with the needle, as a form of art, is a vital and immediate way of letting people express themselves. This is one of the reasons why art is the way it is; multiple artists can tell the same story using the tips of their brushes, but the difference will be that each artist will bring a level of uniqueness and perspective into the story that others would not have been able to see otherwise. With this in mind, everyone has a part of them that lies beneath the surface, waiting to be given wings to find expression

and make its way into the light. Using felting as an artistic way of expressing oneself is beneficial because, through the process of creating something new, people can allow themselves to feel, and express whatever it is that they have within them.

2. Needle felting encourages meditation. Considering that the process of designing and creating new things is intricate, it demands that you concentrate on what you are doing. Because you have to concentrate on one thing and forget about everything that could become distractions (sometimes for a long period), that period can be converted into quality meditation time. During this process also, you will notice that a sense of peace and tranquility comes upon you. This feeling can be traced to the absence of worries and distractions. If you take a closer look at this, this sense of tranquility can be considered the direct result of the first point. Once you can express yourself, you create space in your mind for peace and tranquility.

3. As a further expression of the first point, needle felting is a great way to get rid of depression. There are days when you can feel down, depressed, and not lift a muscle. However, when you pick up a piece

of wool and decide to create something artistic, the knowledge that you have been able to create something out of nothing can be an emotional boost to you. Furthermore, wool and needle felting is one thing you can exercise control over and that way, you can also have the consciousness that some things are still under your care.

Let's not forget the part that sometimes, the knowledge that there is something you can stab, and wouldn't be a problem can be an emotional boost as well. It can give you an avenue to let off some steam, and you can take advantage of that.

**Summary**

1. Felting is simply the creative process of making use of felt (which is a textile material) to create amazing craftworks and art pieces. Needle felting is achieved using a specific kind of needle.

2. Felt, as a fabric, did not come into existence recently. History has it that it has been in existence for as long as can be remembered. Over time, felt has evolved in terms of its use, as people have continually

discovered more advanced ways of putting the fabric to good use.

3. Felt is valuable for a number of reasons. One of the major reasons for this is because it plays a symbolic role in therapeutics. Surprisingly, needle felting is a great way of dealing with depression, even if for a short time interval.

# Chapter 2

## Basic Needle Felting Terminologies

Now that you know what felting is and is all about, and you have seen a few reasons why it is beneficial to your health, it is time for you to be introduced gently into the world of felting.

When it comes to needle felting, there are a few terms that you cannot run away from as they come up every time. These are the jargon associated with this skill and in this chapter, you will be introduced to them.

1. Felt; this is the material that you will be working with. Everything in this book is centered around felts and felting.

2. Fibers; in felting, fibers is constantly being used in place of wool. Fibers is used to describe the processed fleece extracted from sheep. Also, it can be used to distinguish the individual ropes of wool that make up a material; those that you can pull on to and have the wool fabric unravel. A structured

combination of wool fibers will give you a wool fabric (in this context).

3. Fleece; these are the fibers that come straight from their natural sources; the body of sheep. They are unprocessed, and in this context, can not do a lot in terms of usefulness to the individual.

4. Handle; this term is used to describe the texture of a felt piece. It could either be silky, coarse or harsh.

5. Lanolin; this is the naturally occurring grease found in the fleece of many breeds of sheep. This is one reason why fleece is treated after it is taken from sheep; to get this grease off of it. Inasmuch as this grease is present in fleece, Alpaca fleece has been proven to be free of it.

6. Locks; these are unbrushed curls of fleece in their natural forms. Although unbrushed, locks are usually washed and dyed at this stage of their production.

7. Nepps; these are small bits of waste that are usually not discarded. Usually, nepps are collected and used later in the production process of felt as they are used to create wool texture.

8.  Pre-felt; these are partly-completed sheets of felt that have been matted together but have not gone through the last process of shrinking. Because pre-felt has not yet been shrunk (the last process of the felt production process), they are usually heavier than normal felt.

9.  Wool; this is the basic term you should get yourself used to if you will be a successful felt craftsperson. Wool is the processed fleece that has been extracted from sheep. Usually, wool is classified based on the type of sheep that produces it. Usually, when you are going to start with a felting project, you take a look at the kind of wool you will use. For best practices, use finer and softer wool for materials like clothing (stockings, jackets, etc.). On the other hand, coarse wool should be used to create materials at places where they come under constant strain and pressure every day. For example, use coarse wool for creating projects like carpets, doormats, etc.

10. Felting needles; are arguably the most important materials you need to have and know if you will make a great felt craftsperson. Generally, felting needles are long needles that have barns on their

end. This needle is used for interlocking the wool fibers and making sure that your felt remains in good shape for as long as it can be. Considering that the bulk of the work you do with felt is dependent on the needle you are using and your skill with the needle, it is vital that you understand what needles there are, and what you can achieve with all of them. Later in this book, more light will be thrown on the topic of felting needles.

11. Batt; this is a length of pre-felt that has been prepared commercially using a specific machine; the carding machine.

12. Carding; is one of the major processes involved in felting. It is the process of using carders to open up wool for processing, and so that you can be able to see and separate individual wool fibers. Carders, on the other hand, are special tools that look like paddle brushes. They are used to clean fibers or mix different wool types that will be used to make felt together.

13. Fulling; this is one of the final processes involved in felting. Fulling is the process of rubbing the matted and shrunk felt against a rough surface, with the intentions to make the fibers to intertwine as well as

they can, shrink the material and even get smoother than it already is. During fulling, it is your assignment to make sure that your felt comes out as properly as it should and in some cases, you can be permitted to throw the felt around - just a bit (if that's what will do the trick).

14. Micron; this is the unit of measurement of wool fiber thickness. Usually, the number of wool fiber measures on this scale is inversely proportional to the wool fiber's fineness.

15. Nuno felt; this is the name given to a fabric made with wool and laminated with silk. The first step to create this is to lay the wool on the fabric and go about the usual process of rolling the wool with the fabric. As you roll the wool with the silk, wool fibers penetrate the silk, causing both the wool and the silk to start shrinking. The more you roll these and carry out fulling on them, the more they shrink and you get what you want to have.

## Summary

There are a few terminologies you must know before you venture further into creating your first needle felting project. In this chapter, we have taken a look at a few of the most common ones. With them, you can get started with your felting journey.

# Chapter 3

## Top Needle Felting Tips and Tricks

If you are going to make the most out of all your needle felting projects, you must know and apply the tips and tricks that can make you appear like a professional. The thing about tips and tricks is that they help you get the same results you would have gotten if you had worked through the long route (if not better results), and you end up spending less time, energy and resources than you would have spent otherwise.

Here are a few tips and tricks you should have up your sleeves as a person who does needle felting crafts;

1. Felting can be a difficult process, especially if you are still new to it. To give yourself a head start with the process, rub small pieces of wool between your hands like you would a ball of dough. The same way rubbing of dough tends to make it softer, that is the same way your wool will respond when you rub it. Rubbing them tangles the fibers, and they begin to intertwine carefully. When you have done this, you will see that the process of felting becomes easier for

you, as opposed to how it would have been if you had started felting from the beginning without this preparation.

2. As a beginner, there are every chances that you would not be sure of how much wool you will need to complete your projects. With this in mind and to create what you need without experiencing any glitches on the way, there is every possibility that you may end up preparing more wool fabrics than you will need for your project. As a way around this (to prevent the wastage of the extra wool), try starting out the project with small wool. As you progress in the project, prepare more wool and wrap them around the one you are using already.

3. Needles are usually tiny and tend to cave when a lot of pressure is mounted on them. You may have experienced this if you have felted before. To make sure that you do not get stuck in the case that your needle breaks under the pressure that it is put under, you may want to make sure that you have a stash of needles close by. This way, you can easily swap when the need arises.

4.  If you want to create a round, uniform ball of wool, your best bet will be to poke the wool ball in all directions. If you are not looking to create another shape that requires you pay special attention to a part of the ball, a better way to get a ball-shaped object will be to poke evenly in all directions. When you have done this for a while, your ball will begin to take shape.

5.  As you work with your wool, you will discover that the more the ball of wool begins to fall into shape, the more difficult it will be for your needle to pass through easily. A time will come when it may seem that your needle cannot pass through at all. At this point, you can choose to change the size of the needle you are using. Step up the size of the needle to make sure that it can pass through more easily. Conversely, you can slow down with how you poke. Reduce the intensity of your poking. Take your time to pass the needle through the ball of wool. This will take more time as the ball becomes smaller, but it should be able to produce some kind of respite for you.

6.  When you are trying to create a felt project like an animal or pet, you will get to a point where you will

most likely want to include a black, plastic eye. To do this, mark out the spot where you want to add this eye using your needle. After doing this, create holes at that spot using a pair of scissors or an awl. When you have done this, put a bit of glue on the plastic you want to use as the eyes and stick it in the hole you have created. This will take away the stress that you would have gone through if you were going to create the eye from scratch by felting.

7. There is every chance that your needle can break when it is inside the ball of wool. When this happens, carefully press down on the ball of wool but be sure to keep your hands away from where the needle disappeared into. When you have done this and found where the needle disappeared into, carefully use tweezers to pull the needle out.

8. If you find out that you have some unwanted holes in the finished project you are working on, take a piece of wool of the same color, roll it into a ball that can fit into the space that is remaining, and felt it into place over the hole that you have.

9. One way to make your creations cute and more appealing to sight is by adding a face to them. You

may also want to consider adding rosy cheeks to the faces, which can increase people's tendency to be attracted by what you have made.

10. If you are creating an animal or pet with whiskers, one way to easily add whiskers is by sewing them on the face using an embroidery needle and the desired color of thread. This will save you the stress of creating something from scratch and ensure that you end up with the easy whiskers on your creation already.

11. If you are creating something that children will have access to, it is vital that you make it as child-friendly as it can be. To this end, skip using the melamine foam that comes with your kit in your projects. These could cause challenges in the body system if swallowed, so the best thing to do is avoid them altogether. Also, replace the plastic button you would have used as the eyes with a felt material. Create an eye with the needed colors and fit them into the hole you created before for the eyes. When you have finished all these, poke the surface's edges to tuck in the loose fibers of what you have created. You want to make sure that what you are left with is smooth, and does not look rough to the eye. One

easy way to achieve this is by tucking in the rough edges.

12. This is one of the golden rules for felting beginners. Keep it simple. When you initially get started with needle felting, there is every possibility that you would want to go all-in and become the next best thing in one day. However, this may not be the best way of going about things. Better still, start from easier designs and scale up from there. The easier a design is, the easier it will be for you to replicate it and make sure that you get the desired results.

13. As a beginner, you will need a lot of patience. Needle felting is arguably the craft that will require you to stack up as much patience as you can in a box and place it where it is within reach - especially if you are just getting into the craft newly. As a beginner, you will have to create, and at the verge of completing something, discover that you have made a mistake that will demand that you start again. If you are not big on patience, it could be the ruin of something that could have turned out to be something much more for you in the long run.

## Summary

Needle felting is a beautiful craft that you can venture into at any time, and is relatively easy to follow and understand. However, you must be aware of a few tips and tricks that can make the easy journey even easier. These tips and tricks will make you a whiz in needle felting in no time. So, you may want to take notice of them.

# A Short message from the Author:

Hey, I hope you are enjoying the book? I would love to hear your thoughts!

Many readers do not know how hard reviews are to come by and how much they help an author.

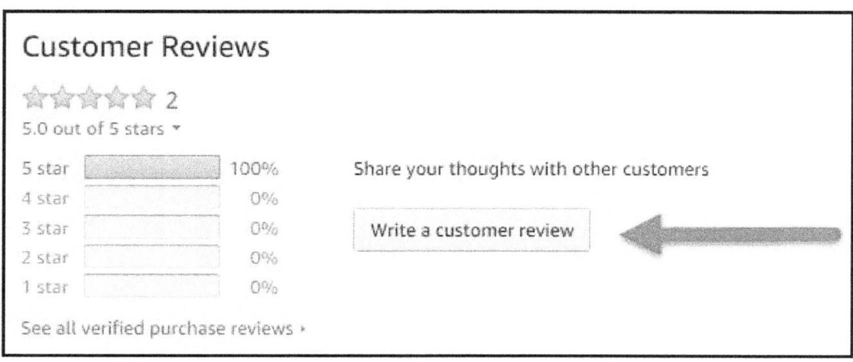


I would be incredibly grateful if you could take just 60 seconds to write a short review on Amazon, even if it is a few sentences!

>> Click here to leave a quick review

Thanks for the time taken to share your thoughts!

# Chapter 4

## Getting Started With Needle Felting

Now, we are beginning to get closer to the heart of the matter.

You have seen what felting is all about and we have been able to talk about a few tips and tricks you should have up your sleeves to make the most of your efforts. Here are a few additional pieces of knowledge that you need to have.

## Basic Tools and Materials Needed

### Wool roving

This is a basic tool required if you will create great felting projects and make the most of your efforts. Roving, simply put, is the wool that has been processed to a large extent, which can be used for felting projects. Many people tend to mistake roving for batts. The major difference between both of them lies in the level to which each has been processed and is ready to be used for felting.

A roving is long, and many times narrow bundle of wool fiber produced as yarn that is spun from wool fleece, raw cotton, or other fibers like fur. Roving is processed wool, passed through the machine to the point that it comes out in long ropes and the fibers are usually more aligned than with other kinds of processed wool. One of the most striking features of roving is that it largely retains its usual natural crimp and smoothness, and this makes it easy for the wool to be used for more detailed projects and projects that require that you use lighter wool. Generally, roving is considered to be fiber that is all ready for spinning and passing through the felting process.

**Felting needle**

This is arguably the most important tool you need as you get started with your felting projects. The process of felting discussed throughout this book is called "needle felting" for a reason; this is because without the needle, you will not be able to achieve anything worthwhile as far as felting is concerned.

Felting needles are a special kind of needles that have wired barbs on their end. These barbs all have one purpose; to get into the wool and cause the wool fabrics' layers to tangle. To achieve this, felt barbs on these needles go in one direction, pulling the layers of the fabric in that direction and they do not return with the layers they have taken from one fabric. When these needles are stabbed into the fabric over a period, the fabric becomes matted up and considered a proper felt. One of the things you need to have in mind as you start making use of these needles is that they are fragile and can cave under some extra pressure. Felt needles are delicate, and if you use the wrong needle for the wrong project, there is every tendency that you will not complete the project with the needle intact. These needles, just like every other needle you can think of, go blunt over time. As you use them to work on your felting projects, a time will come when you will discover that you will need to be more forceful with how you push the needle into the project you are working on for the needle to pass through. You will see that it's not a function of how thick your felting project is becoming. The way around this is to change the felting needle.

For ease of use and to achieve the aims for which they were created, felt needles come in a variety of sizes and shapes. If you are new to needle felting, this assortment of sizes and shapes can be confusing, and you may not know which needle to use and when. Before going further, it is only logical that we look at the different types of needles available and what you can use each of them for.

Felting needles come with different gauge numbers. A gauge number is a representation of how large or small the diameter of your needle is. The higher the number, the larger the needle and vice versa. While larger needles are great because they allow you to do work faster, smaller needles allow your work to come out finely and carefully felted. Depending on the nature of the project at hand, you want to make sure you are using the right gauge.

Another thing you need to notice is the fact that different needles come with different number of barbs. The more barbs on the needle, the quicker and easier it will be for you to felt, and vice versa. However, less barbs are great if you are looking to do work with more fineness and attention to details. Generally, it is advisable that to make the most of your efforts and make sure that you do not spend more time than is necessary on any project, start out with bigger needles (more barbs and a higher gauge number), and reduce the size as you get closer to the end of your project. This way, you do not have to spend so much time on a project, and you can also be sure that you will not turn in a lousy project.

Here is a rundown of the needle sizes, and what each size is most suitable for.

1. 32 gauge; this is a thick and sturdy needle that is most appropriate for working with coarse fibers and pieces that need to be interlocked as tightly as possible. The downside of using this needle for your projects is that it is not the best for neat surfaces and fine details. If those two are prerequisite in what you are doing, this needle may not be the best choice for you to end your project with.

2. 36 gauge; this is also good for doing heavy work. It may not be the best option if you are looking to do something fine and intricate.

3. 38 gauge; this can be seen as the midlander. It is sturdy enough for you to use it in your heavier projects, and it gives a relatively nice finish to your work. While you can get something good at the end of the work you have done, do not stop with this

needle if you have access to other ones that are yet to be discussed.

4.  40 gauge; built for fine work. The strong point of this needle is that you will get a neat job done with it, and that is a win you should look out for. This, though, is not the most appropriate for bulk and coarse materials because the pressure will most likely cause the needle to break in two.

5.  42 gauge; this is reserved for the finest of jobs you can think of. If you are looking to add hair to your projects, make intricate patterns on the felt, or include tiny wisps of wool to the project, they are your go-to options.

## Scissors

Just like every other craft out there, you will need to cut and make shapes out of wool as you felt. This is where scissors come into play. Scissors are necessary to help you cut wool easily. Depending on the nature of the project at hand and the wool's texture, you will need to use a different sized pair of scissors. For example, fabrics that are more coarse and thick naturally need bigger scissors.

## Felting Pad

Next to the needle, the felting pad is the second most important tool you need as you felt. To get the best results, make sure that you have the right mat for your aims. In essence, a felting mat is a dedicated surface where you can carry out the felting creation exercises you want to. It serves as a platform for your project, and makes sure that both your needle and the top of the surface you are working with remain protected from abrasions and other challenges that may arise.

Generally, there are different types of felting mats available for sale. You cannot categorically tell which is better than the other because all of them serve their individual purposes. However, it is vital that before you choose a felting mat, you should pay attention to and make sure that the mat you are about to exchange your bucks for has ticked off a few boxes from the list below.

1. It must have a flat, stable, and smooth surface. You do not want to buy something that has bumps as you begin to use it for your projects.

2. It should be transportable. However, this point is under debate because it is dependent on your needs

and on whether or not you travel a lot. If you are the mobile kind, then you want to make sure that you get a felting mat that is easy to move around.

3.  Your felting mat must be made of a material that is not feltable. You do not want a situation where the needle that pokes the mat also causes it to lose its shape because it is a feltable mat.

4.  Get a mat that is made of a strong material of definite shape and structure. Your mat should be strong enough to withstand pressure (and a lot of that would happen as you begin to make use of the mat), so you need to be sure that you have that in mind as you make the decision to buy a mat.

Here are the types of mats available to you and from which you can make your choice.

A. Brush mat

Brush mats are most suitable for needle felting. Generally, this kind of mat looks like a hairbrush and is great because the bristles of the mat hold the wool in place, giving you the leverage to work on the project without having to stop every second to readjust and rearrange the wool.

As a best practice, you may want to take a thin layer of cloth and place it on top of the mat's bristles. This is to prevent the mat from holding on top of your wool as you felt and cause dents you do not want to have on the wool. Brush mats are made like this because the bristles of the mat are great to keep the wool you are working with in place, and they do not hold on to your felting needle in the case that your needle makes contact with the mat.

While the brush mat is handy, it has a major downside. This is the fact that brush mats are usually small, and are not suitable for larger-sized projects. Also, if you use this mat for a long period, there is every tendency that it will cause your hands to begin to itch and get painful. Make use of this mat when the need arises, but be sure that you are not going to use it for bulky projects, and that you wouldn't be using the mat for a prolonged period at the same time.

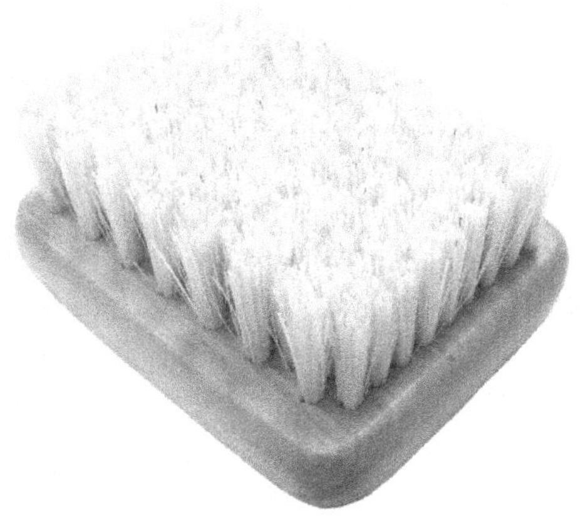

B. Styrofoam felting mat

This mat is made of Styrofoam and is most suitable for lightweight projects. If you must make use of Styrofoam be sure that it is a Styrofoam mat, and not just Styrofoam. While this mat is great because it offers stability and comfort with your work, it is not the best option in the long run because Styrofoam is feltable. What this implies is that the more you make use of this mat for your projects, the more likely it will be for it to start getting out of shape. Also, the worse it becomes, the harder it gets for you to use this mat for your projects. In general, make use of this mat as a last resort.

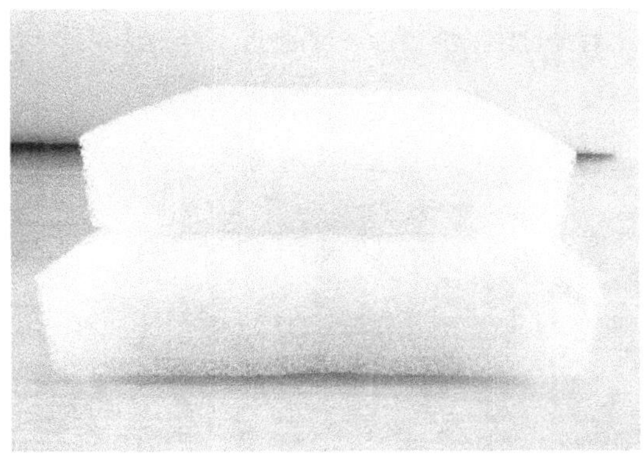

## C. Sponge felting mat

These mats are easily mistakable for Styrofoam mats because they have the same look if you are to look at them superficially. A perfect sponge felting mat does not have the regular sticky and somewhat heavy feel of a normal sponge, although it is built to withstand some amount of pressure. The good thing about the sponge mats is that they are thicker than the Styrofoam mats and as such, you can be comfortable to work with the mat on your mat (but remember to be careful, so you don't hurt yourself). Sponge mats come in a variety of sizes and colors, and they are noiseless when you use them for felting.

Other reasons you may want to consider using this kind of sponge is because they have the possibility of fastening something to them, and they are also comfortable to be used.

## Additional Tools and Materials (Optional)

Now that we have quickly gone through the materials you must have if you will be successful with your felting project, there are other materials that you need. These, however, are not as important as those that have been discussed in the last section, and even without them, you can create a great project.

However, they would be great additions to your toolkit.

**Needle holders**

A felt needle holder is a tool that is used to provide a firm grip on the felt needle. Considering that felting requires a lot of energy and pressure to be mounted on the needle, there is a need for your hands to be protected so that they do not poke your hands and cause wounds. The needle holders are usually wooden, and can fit into any of the felting needles - irrespective of the size of the needle involved. For further protection, you can switch up the sides of the needle so that the sharp side stays in the enclosure of the needle holder. This way, you protect yourself and the needle from getting spoilt easily.

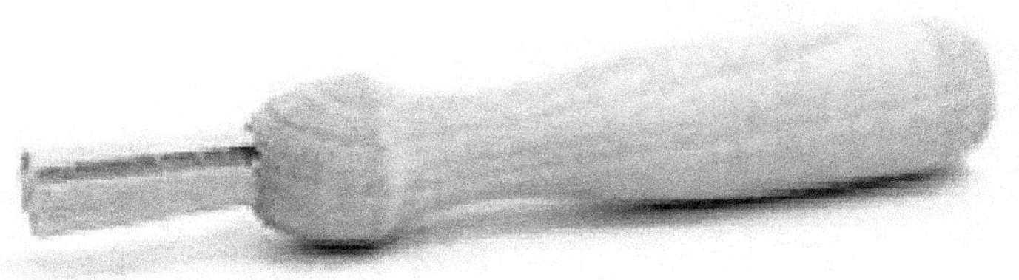

## Carding brushes

Carding is a basic practice in felting. It is the process by which you combine available wool colors, with the aid of hand carders or carding brushes, with the intent to create new colors that were not available before. Carding allows you the luxury of having more options than you would have, if you did not have the option of carding.

Carding brushes are the simple implements that you can use to carry out the carding exercise.

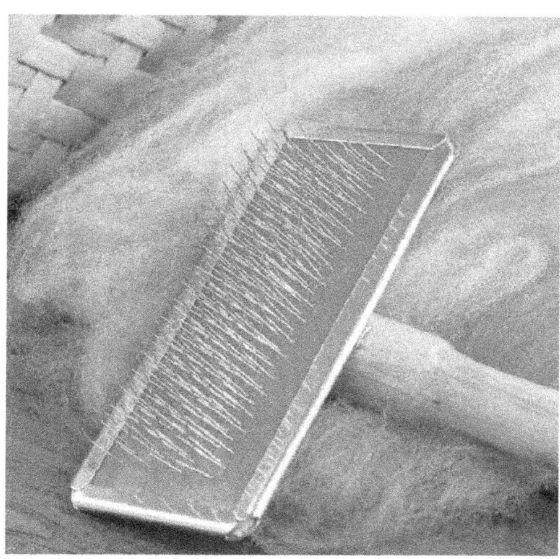

**Formers**

Depending on the shape you are trying to create, and the project you are working on, sometimes it may be better for you to have something which you can wrap the wool around before you begin stabbing it. That is what formers is used for. Formers aim to give the wool some kind of definition so that while you poke it, you do not have to be afraid that the shape it is bending into would not be what you need.

For this, you can make use of a number of equipment lying around your house. Wooden spoon handles, toothpicks, skewers, etc. are all examples of what you can use as formers. This is the great news; you do not have to wait until you have the exact material you need (former). Begin with something lying around your house that can solve the problem, and work from there.

**Summary**

There are several tools you need if you are going to have the best of experiences as you felt. You must figure out these tools and make sure that you have all of them at hand, even before you get started with any of your felting projects. This way, you do not start with a project and get stuck halfway.

# Chapter 5

## Crafting Needle Felting Projects

Now that you have all the foundational knowledge to get you set up the right way and give you a head start as a felting expert, it is time for us to take a quick look at a few easy projects that you can embark upon all by yourself.

By following the ideas discussed in this book to the letter, you should be able to create your own project in record time.

Here they go.

**Felted Strawberries**

These are easy-to-make, DIY strawberries. You can make the regular strawberries, or you can make the ones that have a happy face painted on them. With the right tools and knowledge, you can be done with yours in no time. Follow these steps to make your felt strawberry;

**Supplies you need**

A. Felt scraps colored green and red.
B. Seed beads (depending on the number of strawberries you want to make. However, you should have at least two dozen at hand).
C. Craft glue.
D. Regular sewing thread. You should also have a strong thread as you will need it as the felt begins to get stronger.
E. Stuffing for the strawberries.

## Directions

A. Start by making the pattern for the strawberry. To accomplish this, draw a half-circle on a piece of paper and cut it out. Also, draw a strawberry leaf on the paper and cut it out. The strawberry leaf should look like a star with multiple edges.

B. Pin the half-circle you cut out to a scrap of red felt. The leaf goes to a scrap of green felt and trace out the felt that way so that you have felt of those shapes and sizes.

C. Fold the circle you now have in half so that the straight sides lie, one against the other. When you have aligned the straight sides, stitch them together. At this point, you should have something like this;

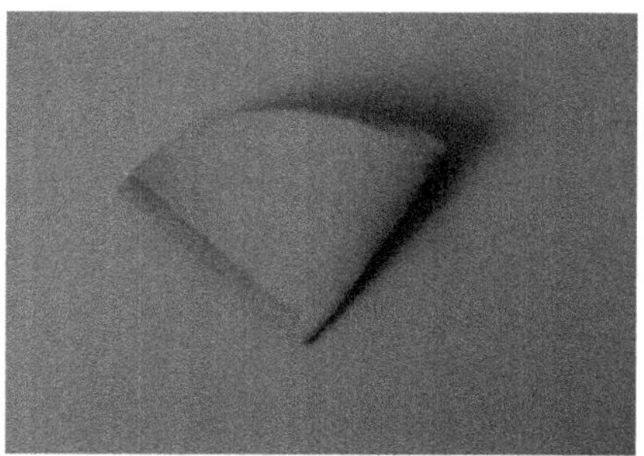

D. Turn what you have stitched right side out. You should have something shaped like the top part of a funnel. Stuff this with the stuffing material you kept aside, and with the strong thread you have, sew the top closed. To do this., make a running stitch at the top and pull the stitch when you are done with it to close the top of what you have. If you tug the top closed and you feel there is still some space, in the sense that you can still stuff some filling inside, by all means, do so until you have something full. It should look this way at this point;

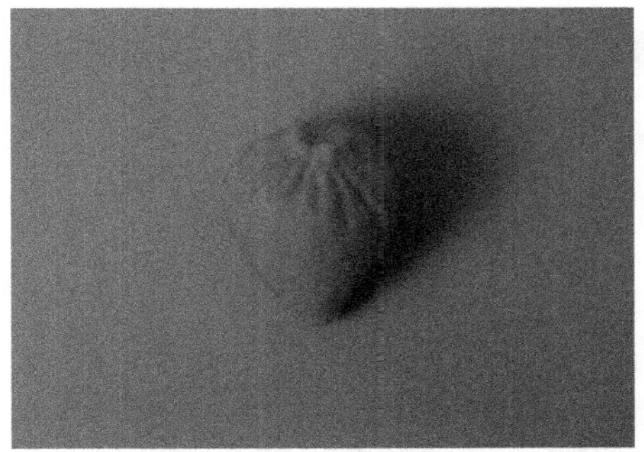

E. Thread a small needle with the sewing thread you have. Insert this needle at the top of the strawberry and pull it out by the side. Insert a seed bead into the thread that you pulled out by the side, and pass the thread through the side of the strawberry it just came out from. Repeat this process until you have put enough seed beads at all sides of the strawberry. When you are done, tie off the thread, hiding the knot near the top of the strawberry and squeeze a ring of craft glue along the top of the strawberry.

F. Place the leaf on top of the glue and leave it to dry. To make sure it stays in the right place as the glue dries, use pins to hold it down. When this is done, take out the pins and enjoy what you have created.

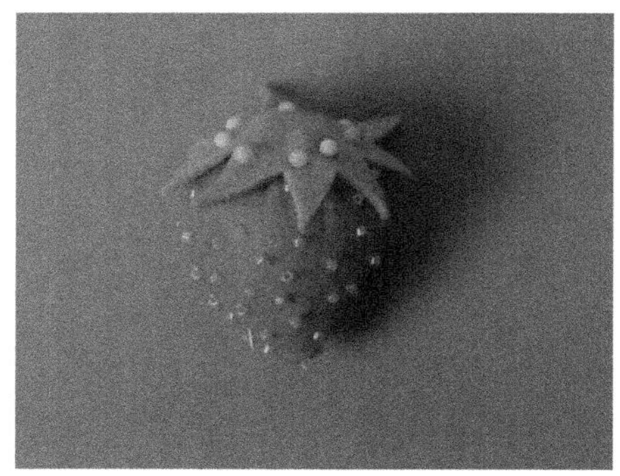

## Felted Dog

This is another project you can embark upon as a beginner with limited knowledge on how to carry out more complicated felting tasks.

## Supplies you need

A. Roving (in your choice of colors).
B. Pipe cleaners to be used as the body frame.
C. Needle felting mat, needles and a needle holder.
D. Picture of the chosen dog, so that you have something to look at.
E. Beads for the eyes, or glass eyes if you have those.
F. Sharp scissors.
G. Wire cutters or tweezers.

**Directions**

A. Start by felting the head of the dog. To achieve this,
   follow these steps;

- Pull off a group of roving from that of the base color
  of the dog. Roll this into a ball.
- Lay the ball on the mat and start pushing your
  needle through it to felt it. A 38 gauge needle is
  good for this step. Poke the needle through the ball
  in a straight way, up and down but be careful and
  look out for your hands. Push the needle through
  the roving as far as it can go before taking it out
  again.

B. Shape the muzzle and the forehead of the dog. After
   you have given the head some definition and shape,
   it is time for you to make the muzzle of the dog
   become prominent. To do this,

- Punch your felting needle in a straight line across
  the centre of the ball you have created. Because you
  are looking to get this shape on one side of the ball,
  do not do it all way round; just one side of the ball
  will do.

- Keep punching this until it begins to take a stronger and more compact shape around that side of the ball. Don't work this area too much. All it needs to get to is this shape.

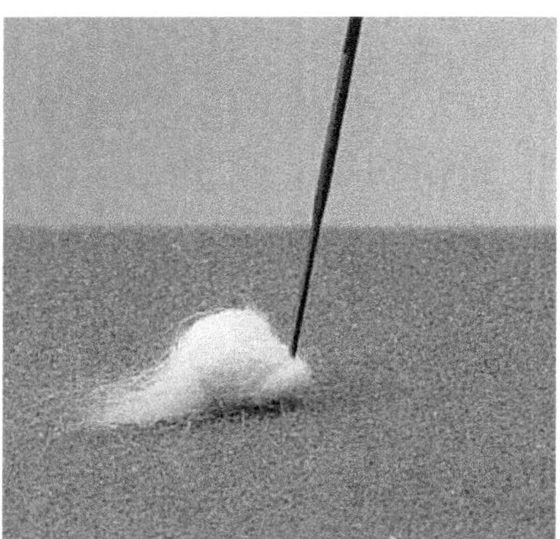

- While you punch, pay close attention to the shape of what you have. The aim is to make sure that you get something that is more rounded at the edge and that broadens out towards the back, just like the shape of the dog's head is.

C. Make ears for your dog

- Gather two small 1/4 to 1/2 inch balls of fleece in the color you want to use for the ear of your dog. Make sure that these quantities are the same.

- Begin to punch through with your needle until what you have gathered begins to take up the shape of a triangle or oval. This is dependent on the shape you want for the ears of your dog. To spice things up a bit, you can include some colored fleece in the dog's ears to make the ears have different colors.
- When you have created the ears, felt them to the dog's head, and make sure that you do that in the right position. Follow the felting guidelines by placing the ear against the spot of the head you want to insert it into and felt into place.

D. Create a nose for the dog

- Take a small black fiber ball and fit in place at the tip of the nozzle that you shaped in the first stage of your project.
- For best practices, begin to punch from the edges, and work your way around until you have felted the nose to the head of the dog. Be careful to avoid the center of the nose you created, as working at the center can drastically reduce the nose's size.

E. Create the body of your dog

- Cut lengths of the pipe you have to create the body of your dog. Ideally, 3mm thick pipes will do, and you need to make sure that color of the pipe and the color of the dog's body are the same.
- Follow the measurement of the dog you are modeling, and scale it down to the small size you have to work with. For best practices, cut pipes that are 1/4 inch longer than double the measurement of the scale you are working with. This will give you enough room to work with.
- Form the body frame by wrapping the front leg section around the part of the body section that is 1/4 inch away from the end of the pipe you cut. The back leg should go to any point that is the correct scale distance away from the front legs' point.

F.  Add a base coat of fiber to the body

- Cover the body frame you have created with a thin coat of fiber and wrap this fiber around the body frame with some thin thread and your felting needle.
- When you are done, begin needle felting the body. Because of the plastic under, you want to be cautious as you do this. When the needle has grazed the top of the frame, pull it back up to begin the

felting process. Have in mind that you need to pay attention while you do this. Your aim is to make sure that you have an even coat of felted fur covering the dog when you are done.

G. Fix the head of the dog to the body you have created

- Place your dog's head a bit above the place where the front legs are. Make sure that the soft, unfelted area of the head lies against the trunk of the dog. As much as it lies within you, spread this unfelted area all around the sides of the dog so that when you are done, you will have something evenly spread.
- With a coarse felting needle, work the head and the body together as this is how you felt the head to the body. Stop felting when the head is firmly held up where you want it to be.

H. Attach a tail to your dog

- Create a tail from some roving fiber of the color you want. Roll this into the form of a thin cylinder and felt it into the shape you want it to be in.
- When you have the shape and size of the tail you want, needlefelt it to the dog's body that you have

created. Use the same method you used to add the head of the dog to its body.

I.  Finally, double-check to make sure that you got the project right. If your model dog is there, take the measurements and look through your scale once again. This makes sure that you create the right kind of project. Needle felt the stray patches of roving sticking out the dog's sides into shape and making the final markings to your dog. When you are done with this, trim the coat on your dog, and if you see the need to, create further designs on it with some color painting.

J.  Add the eyes by gluing them to the right position at the front of the head. This is the easiest way to add the eyes.

At the end, you should have something of this nature;

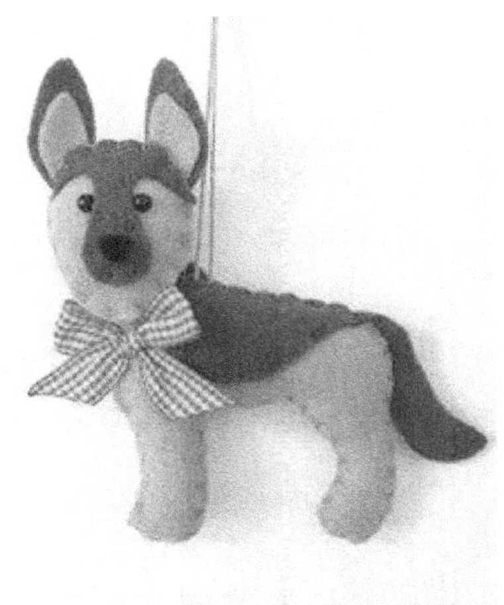

## Felted Buttons

This is especially valuable if you are looking for something to do with a button to make it appear better than it already is. However, you must understand the steps involved so that you do not make a mistake with the project you want to work on. Here is how you can make a simple felted button.

## Supplies you need

A. Wool roving of the colors you need.
B. Felting supplies (needle and mat)
C. Wool yarn (the same color of the cloth the button is meant for).

**Directions**

A. Take some of the wool roving you want to use for the button and shape it into a circle with a diameter of about 5cm. If you are not sure of the measurements, just take as much roving as you think is needed for the button and wrap it into the appropriate size.

B. Start poking the wool you have bunched up with your felting needle. Depending on the shape you want the button to have, you may want to concentrate on some parts of the button. Just know that the areas you poke the more will come out flatter and more compact than the other areas.

C. Keep up with the poking until the wool is firm and has shaped into the size you want it to have. If you notice a part of the wool not being the way you want it to be, be sure to shape it by poking the right side a few times.

D. For the signature button shape, poke the circle more in the center. This will force the center to shrink in further, leaving you with something that looks a lot like your regular buttons.

E. In the center of the button you have felted, create four holes with a needle. This is wool, so all you need to do is poke the center of the button at the desired spots until you have the hole pressed through.

If done correctly, you should have something of this nature;

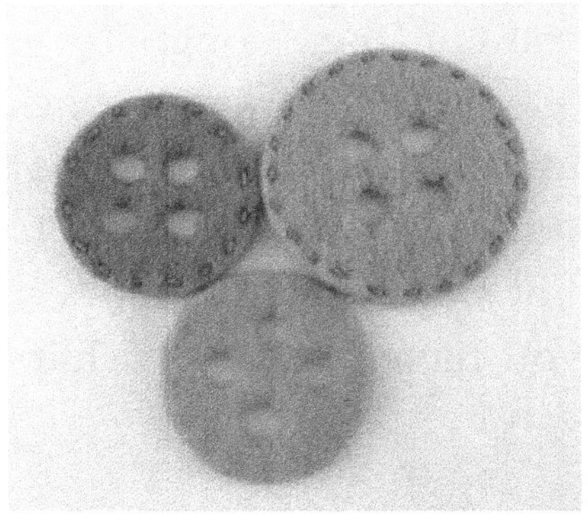

## Felted Owls

These are a delight to add to your ever-growing stash of little felt arts. Here's how you can create a felted owl, even if you are a beginner.

**Supplies you need**

A. Felting supplies (needle, mat, needle clamp/holder)
B. Felt roving of the desired colors
C. Scissors

**Directions**

A. Pull off a part of the roving of the color you want the owl's body to be in and roll it into a little ball. What you pull off should be enough for the owl's body, but if it is not, you can always go back and add more roving. Ensure that the shape as you fold comes out round and not oval or cylindrical. To make sure of this, fold the sides toward the center and keep folding till you have gotten the shape and size you need.

B. Lay down the ball you have created on the felt mat and begin to felt by poking it in all sides with the needle. Make sure your needle gets to the center of the ball as you poke, and not all the way through. Also, poke from all directions to not have a misshapen thing at the end of the felting process.

C. Flatten one side of the ball by felting upwards. This flatter side of the ball will serve as the owl's base on which you can keep it to sit.

D. Get a piece of wool in a lighter shade. This will be for the stomach of the owl. Felt it into position by poking straight down and into the main body you have created. If you want to add other colors, follow this process and do the same at the different parts of the body you want to add colors to. However, you want to be careful so that you do not create something ridiculous, and that cannot pass for an owl.

E. Add the eyes of the owl. To achieve this, take some pieces of white roving and roll them into little balls. Felt these balls into position at the top of the owl and be sure that they are stuck well in place.

F. Start work on the beak of the owl. To achieve this, get a piece of beak-colored wool (which is usually golden brown). Roll this into a tiny cone with your fingers and felt it between the eyes and the belly. For best practices, felt this directly under the eyes, and not too far away from there at most. While creating the beak, pay some attention to the beak's tips so that they can come out as pointy. To achieve this pointy shape, felt the tips of the beak by poking from the sides. This will make sure that it does not come out as flat as the eyes and the patch that you added beneath to signify the owl's belly.

G. Create the irises of the owl by making use of black roving. Pull off the tiniest amount of roving, roll it into a ball and felt it in the center of the white patch you created earlier for the eyes. To make sure that you get the best result at this stage, start felting from the edges. Felting from the middle may be counterproductive because it can reduce the size of the iris you want the owl to have and this black portion must be of reasonable quantity.

H. Trim the sides of the owl that you have created and set it up with others. This is a picture of what a felted owl looks like;

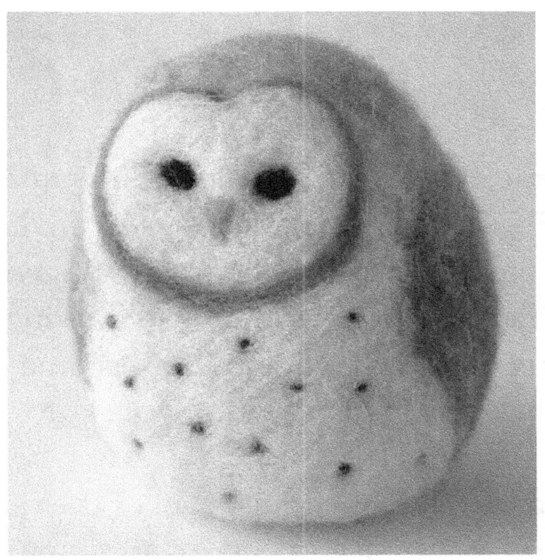

## Felted Cats

If you are a lover of cats and would love to have miniature felt cats lying somewhere around you, you may want to give this a trial. Follow the simple steps detailed here to create your felt cat in a little while.

## Supplies you need

A. Felting materials (mat, needle, needle holder, etc).
B. Wool roving of different colors.
C. Sponge block.

## Directions

A. Take some roving of the color you want your cat to be in. Roll it into a loose ball and make sure that there is some space between your fingers. With the felting needle, stab the rolled roving from all directions till you have gotten the shape of a tightly packed ball. This is the head of your cat.

B. Get a larger piece of felting wool of the same color as the head. Wrap it into an oval shape with your hands and make sure that it is loose enough. To make sure that there is some definition in this part of the cat (which is the body), you may want to add some stuffing to it. This will make sure that it is puffy and has some kind of definition.

C. Attach the head to the body of the cat that you have created. Take the head and place it at the desired angle you want it to be with respect to the body. Take care however, because once you have joined these two parts, there won't be much you will be able to do with them again in terms of adjustment. Attach the head and the body by stabbing all around the neck area till the knots are tight enough.

D. To make limbs for your cat, go through the same process through which you created the body. However, this time, make sure that you are making use of much smaller pieces because the limbs should not be as large as the body. Make four of these and set them aside.

E. Go through the same process through which you attached the head and body together to attach the limbs to the body. Take care to make sure that you attach the limbs at the right places on the body to not end up with mismatched limbs or unequal limbs.

F. Create a tail for your cat. Take just enough roving for this and wrap it into the shape of a cylinder. Stab the cylinder you have crested again and again with the needle until the shape is set. Attach the tail to the rear end of the cat.

G. Create ears for your cat by taking the desired color of roving and folding it into a triangular shape. Stab this triangle from the sides to ensure that they stay in place and attach them at the right parts of the head (at either side of the upper part of the cat's head).

H. Make eyes for your cat by rolling black roving into two small balls and felting them into position on the face. Be sure that the distance between the eyes is optimum and that they do not look too big for the cat's size.

I. Add a little beauty to the cat you have created by adding a little color. From another ball of roving, get little quantities and felt them at the right positions on the cat's body.

J. Trim the cat and cut out excess strands of roving that may be poking out from different parts of the body. You can adjust the cat to change its posture. Set up the complete project at a vantage spot where you can see what you have created.

Here's what you should have at this point;

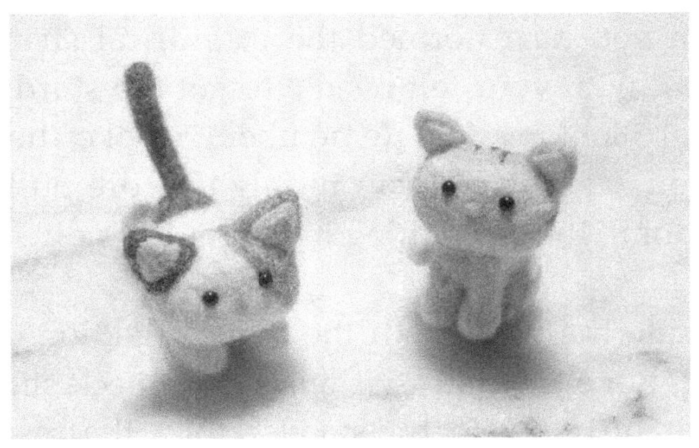

## Felted Mouse

This is an easy-to-do felt project. To carry this out,

## Supplies you need

A. Wool roving of all the desired colors.
B. Felt supplies.

## Directions

A. Get just enough roving that you will need for the mouse's body and roll them into a cylindrical shape. This method is easy because you do not need to do a lot of work to come up with your mouse.

B. When you have formed the cylindrical shape, start poking with your felt needle to get the sturdy shape you are looking for. Remember to poke the roving till you are just halfway through before pulling out and doing the same thing in the mouse's directions.

C. Separate the head from the body by doing one tiny thing. Poke the part that will be the neck slightly so that it turns out a bit smaller than the rest of the wool you have. This will separate the wool head from the rest of the body.

D. Start working on creating the limbs for your mouse. The processes are the same for creating limbs for your mouse and creating limbs for a cat. The only difference will be in the sizes of the limbs. The limbs of the mouse will be smaller than that of the cat.

E. Attach the limbs to the parts of the body where they should be inserted. Two of the limbs should be added under the body; these are the feet. The other two should be added to the upper sides of the rabbit. These are the upper limbs. As a best practice, you may want to stick a needle in the limbs to create a little definition in them while you attach them to the mouse's body.

F. Create the ears of your mouse by making two oval shapes from roving. At the center of these shapes, felt some roving of another color. Create two of these and attach them to the head's top sides by the same process of felting.

G. If you think it necessary, you may cover the entire piece with some white roving. This will help make sure that your work looks neat and organized.

H. At the center of the face, felt the nose. This should be done with a triangular-shaped, pink-colored roving. With black wool, outline the lower half of the nose and continue this downward in a single line; this is the muzzle. At the lower part of the muzzle, spread the line out into the two sides of the face.

I. Felt the other parts of the face as you go on. The shape of the face is that it is usually smaller at the nose's tip and widens out as you go back towards the head's back. With this in mind, keep felting the head from all directions and adjust the size and shape of the head of your mouse as you go.

J. Gum two of the black eyes you have at the required positions on the face with some glue.

K. If you see the need to add more designs on the mouse, please do so but make sure that you remain within the boundaries of what a mouse looks like in real life. You do not want to create something that looks nothing like a mouse.

L. Create and felt the tail to the back of the mouse you have.

At this point, you should have something like this;

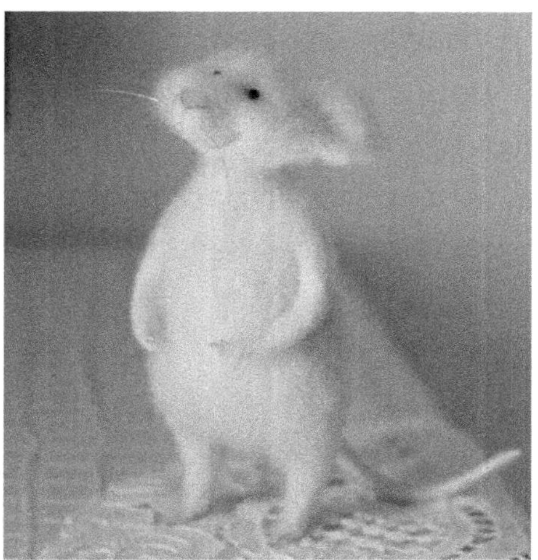

## Mini Decorative Pillow

This is a great project for you to embark upon because it is simple to make and has many uses. Follow these steps to create yours;

## Supplies you need

A. Needle and thread.
B. Felt.
C. Gum.
D. Some fillers to stuff the pillow with (toilet paper, stuffing, light foam, whatever can serve is acceptable).
E. A meter rule.

## Directions

A. Start by cutting the fabric that you will use. This will be a part of the felt that you want to use as the pillow cover. This will be rectangular in shape, and you will fold it over again during the pillow's creation. So, you want to make sure that you do not cut something too small.

B. Fold the piece of felt that you have cut out in half and start by sewing the two edges lying over themselves together.

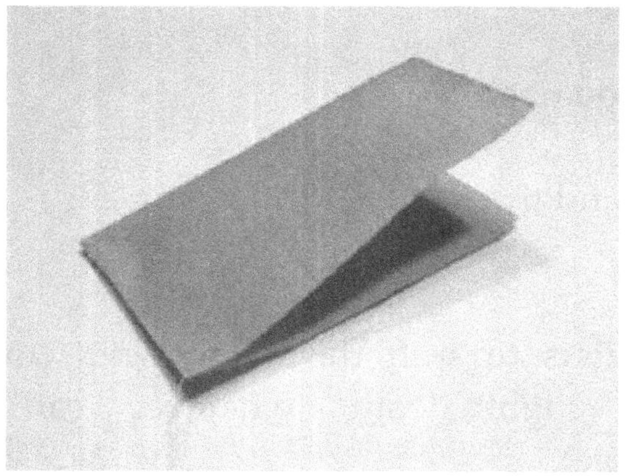

C. With a blanket seal, seal the first two edges together. After sealing the edges, turn the pillow material inside out (the right side facing out). After that, stuff your filling into the pillow and titch the other side of the pillow using invisible stitching.

D. When you are done with the invisible stitching, you are basically done with the pillow. Decorate it with other pieces of felt or whatever you have designed for this purpose and enjoy your pillow.

You should have something like this;

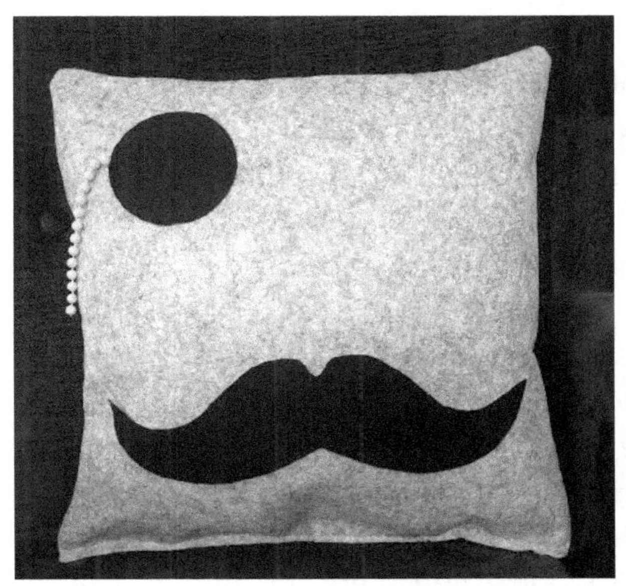

## Felt Fat Plants

These are a beautiful and easy-to-do kind of plants. With them, you can decorate almost any surface you can think of.

## Supplies you need

A. Extra fine merino wool
B. Carded maori wool
C. Foam rubber
D. Felt needle

E.  Warm water
F.  Soap
G. Bubble wrap
H. Scissors
I.  Thin foam sheet

**Directions**

A. Spread a piece of the foam rubber you have on the surface you are working and place a merino wool circle on it. Let the merino wool be about 20cm large.

B. On the merino wool, carefully lay two other layers of maori wool. Align them to the edges of the merino wool you placed at first and make sure that the center remains untampered with. For best practices, let the two layers you just added be of wool that is a different color from the merino you set down at first.

C. Cover all these layers with two layers of merino once again. At this point, you should have about four layers of wool laid upon themselves.

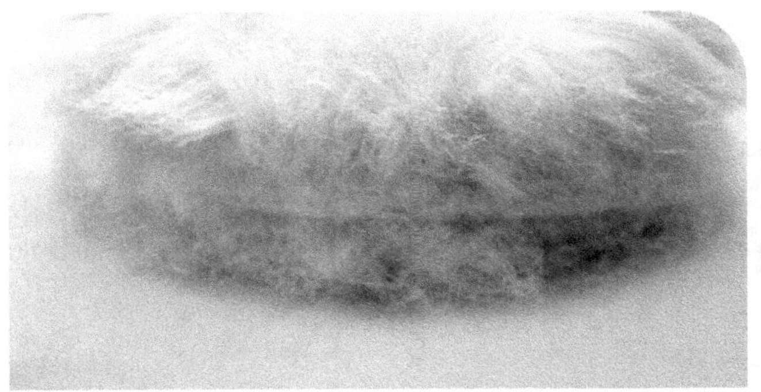

D. Lay on top of all these layers, a 25cm x 25cm square of foam sheet and make sure that this sheet has a hole of about 5cm diameter in the middle. Ensure that the middle of the foam sheet matches the middle of all the wool you laid out underneath it.

E. Repeat steps A to C, but this time make sure that all you are placing goes on top of the foam sheet.

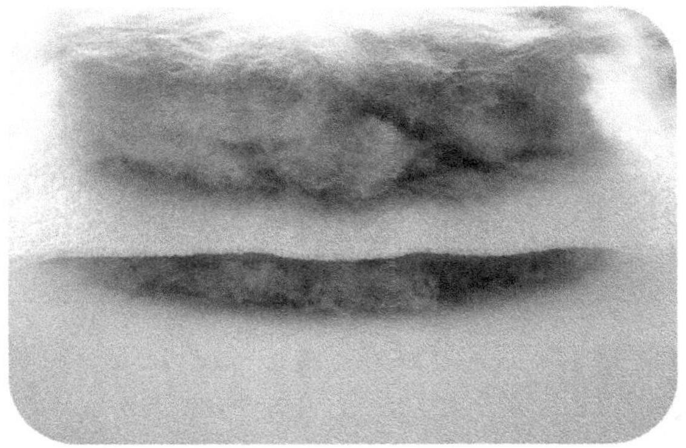

F. With a felt needle, attach the middle of all the layers of wool you have added. When you are done with this, take the foam rubber away and place the wool on the bubble wrap you have.

G. Sprinkle soapy water on the wool to get it wet. With a piece of bubble wrap, cover the wet wool and press down on the bubble wrap until the wool is totally wet; both on top and under it. Roll the material you have and start rubbing back and forth on it. Continue this process until you have shrunken the wool by at least 30% (or significantly if you do not get the percentage usage). This is how you should roll it.

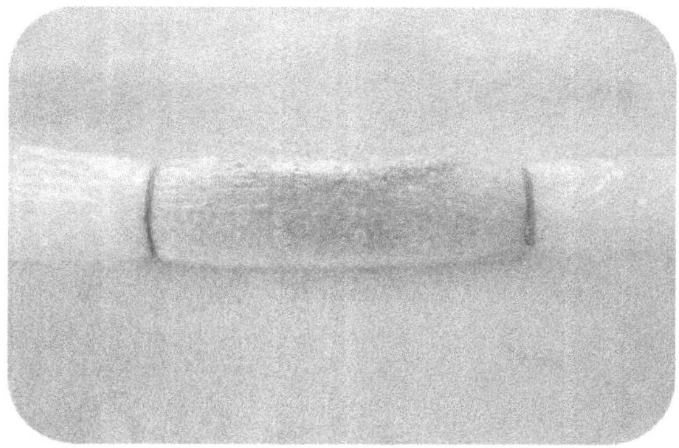

H. When you are done with rolling, remove the bubble wrap and get the excess water off the wool, which is now of a reduced size.

I.  From the edges, cut the petals of your plant. They may be of different sizes and shapes. However, the aim here is to make sure that you get as creative as you can and do not get to the center with what you are cutting. This way, you do not run the risk of having your plants fall off. After cutting the petals, wet the plant again, roll it further until it has reduced further in size.

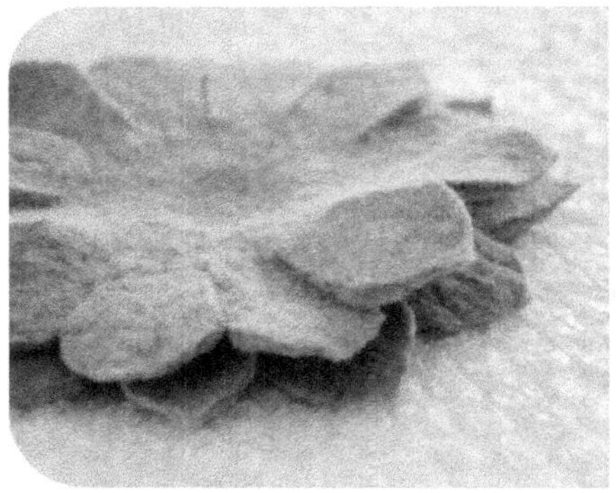

J.  Bunch up the plant in your hands and rub as if it were a ball. Continue this until the plant has felted properly. Choose a pot for the plant and set it up in the pot. You can further choose how you want to set up your plant. In any case, you are done with the main work and all you have left is to make it as creative as it can get. Enjoy setting up your plant where you can always see it, for the sake of how beautiful it looks.

If you have done this project correctly, you should have something of this nature;

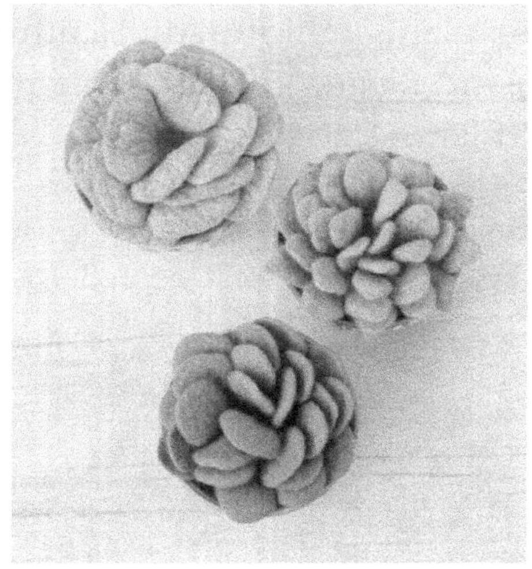

**Felt Ball Earrings**

These are very simple to create, and when done well, it can help you step up the classy look you want to pull off for any event.

**Supplies you need**

A. Wood felt balls (about 1/2 inches in size). You can purchase these online.
B. Some hot glue and glue gun.
C. 10mm posts.

**Directions**

A. On the post you have, squirt some glue with the glue gun.

B. Press the felt ball on the glue that you have squirted on this post and hold it down to allow the glue hold on to the ball.

C. That's it. You have created a simple felt ball earring that you can wear for any event.

D. Conversely, if you cannot find any already-made felt balls, you can walk through the process of creating yours if you have the desired color of roving. Just go through the process described in earlier sections of this chapter and make your own felt ball. When you have your ball, follow the steps outlined above to create your earring.

This is what these earrings look like.

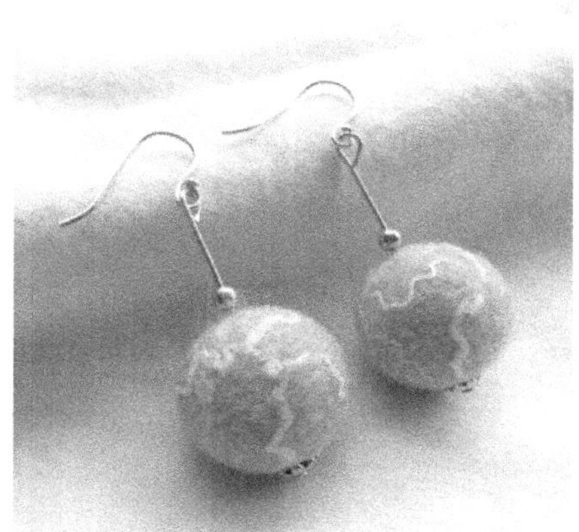

**Felt Pin-Cushion**

This is a simple felt idea that you can try out with your child if you are a parent or a guardian. It is simple to work around and if done well, should be able to absorb your little one until the project is done. The beautiful part of this is that you can decide to switch things up a bit by changing the cushion's shape and working your way around the new shape you want your pillow to take up.

Here's how you go about it;

**Supplies you need**

A. Felting materials
B. Roving of different colors
C. Needle and a strong thread

**Directions**

A. Get two batches of felt; one in another color and the other in white.

B. From the first felt piece that you want to use as the primary felt piece, cut out 2 round shapes and one strip from it.

C. Combine the strip end by stitching them together.

D. Attach one of the round pieces you have created to the bottom of the strip. Use a simple sewing technique for this.

E. After sewing, stuff the finished product with some stuffing to get it into the shape you want for it to be.

Stitch the top round piece when you are done with this step.

F.  Make some kind of patterned design out of the other felt piece you have in the beginning. To make the design, simply cut out the shape you want it to be in and felt this to any chosen part of the cushion you have created. Conversely, you can choose to felt it to the cushion if that is what works for you.

This is what your felt pin-cushion looks like

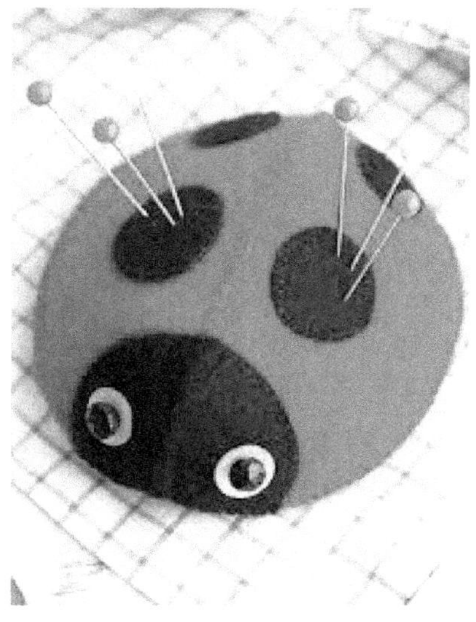

**Felt Corsage**

This is a great project you may want to try out if you are the kind of person that goes out a lot. It is also kid-friendly and you can get your child to be involved in the process if you have one. It is easy to make, and by following the outlined steps, you should have your corsage in no time.

**Supplies you need**

A. Bright-colored felt pieces.
B. Scissors
C. Hot glue and a glue gun
D. Buttons
E. Needle and thread

**Directions**

A. Get the felt pieces that you have and cut them into flower shapes. These pieces must be of different colors, but do not include colors that will end up as a disaster to the eyes. You want to make sure that you have done your color selection properly.

B. Get another felt piece and from there, cut a smaller piece of flower petal. This will be used to add a little detail to the corsage you want to make.

C. With your glue and the glue gun, you will stick the corsage petals together; big one to small one. Just hold the petals the way you want them to be and squirt some of the glue in the right place. Position the smaller petal you have created on the glue and hold these two positions until they have set together. Continue this process for as many petals as you want to work on.

D. You can enhance your corsage's looks by stitching on a button to the center of the flower that you have created. When you are done with this, put pins at the back of the corsage so it can be worn as a brooch, or you can place a ribbon around it so that it can be worn as an armband. In any case, there are a few options as to what you will do with the corsage you have created.

Here is what the corsage looks like;

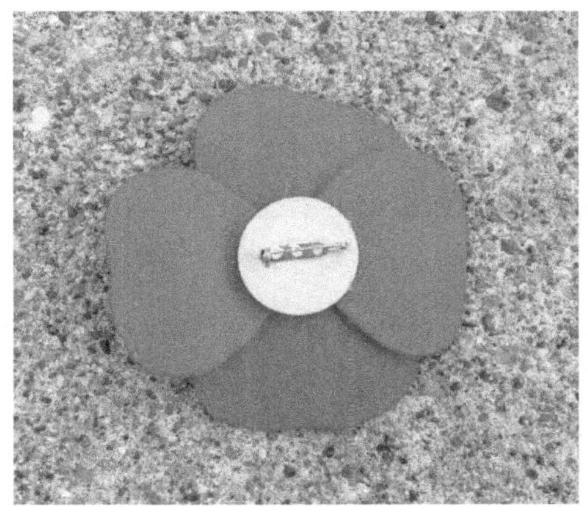

## Felt Coasters

This is a great project to consider if you are a parent and looking for something to absorb your child with. It is easy to make and comes out quite beautiful if done well. If you have a child of the appropriate age, you may want to consider involving him in this creative process that is very easy for him.

## Supplies you need

A. Felt materials.
B. Felt
C. A pair of scissors
D. Hot glue and glue gun
E. Small beads
F. Needle and thread.

**Directions**

This is pretty much easy to do. Just

A. From the felt you have, cut out circles of different sizes. Some should be bigger and the other ones smaller. Ensure that the circles you are cutting out can be fit against themselves, and that they will do so properly.
B. With the glue gun, squirt some glue on top of the bigger circle and fit smaller circles on top of the bigger ones. Hold these in place and allow them to dry. To make the coaster appear bigger and more beautiful, you can add up to three circles in one coaster, but make sure that all circles are of different sizes.

C. With your needle and thread, fix the small beads at intersections between circles on the coaster. This helps make it look better. To do this, all you need to do is pass the needle through the coaster and slip a bead through. Pass the needle through the coaster next to where the first bead entered to hold it in place, and do the same for as many beads as you want to join. To switch things up a little, use beads of different colors, but be sure that you are not using too many beads.

D. Lay out the coaster you have created, and make sure that it is smooth. If it does not have a smooth look, you can consider switching it up a bit by trimming with your scissors or adjusting with the felt needle you have.

Your coasters should look like these

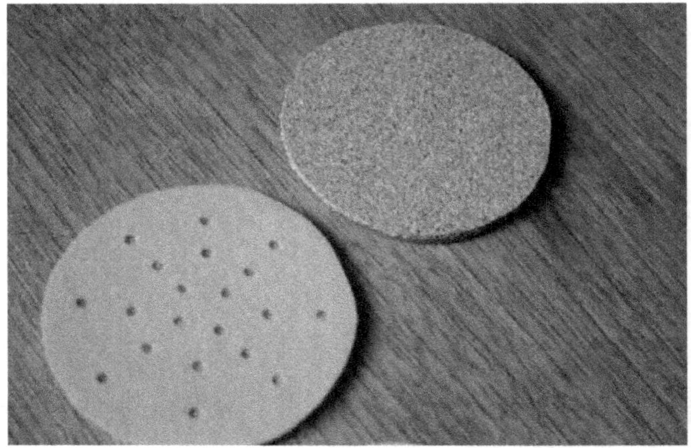

**Felt Eye Mask**

This is a simple project you can embark upon at any time. Eye masks are necessary, especially if you are sensitive to light when you sleep as they will keep unnecessary glare out of your eyes. Although the main material used in making this mask may not be the felt, felts still play a vital role in the mask because they form the inner part of the mask.

To create your felt eye mask, here are the steps you need to follow;

**Supplies you need**

A. Thread and needle
B. 1/4 inch elastic band.
C. Felt fabric or lining for the mask
D. Something heavy to act as a filler for the mask.
E. Pair of scissors and other felt supplies.

**Directions**

A. Make a print of the mask you want to create on a piece and pin this piece to the fabric you are using for the mask. Print the piece on the fabric and cut it out. This piece could be paper or whatever with which you can create a print. Print the felt lining as well and keep these aside.

B. It is time for you to measure out your elastic and begin to assemble all the pieces. To do this;

• Hold one end of the elastic at the outside end of your right eye. Stretch this gently and pull the elastic around the back of your head until you reach the outer edge of your left eye. This is the spot you should cut out and use this length for the mask you are creating.

C. Place one side of the mask on a table with the right side facing up. Pin one side of the elastic to the right side of the mask and the other to the mask's left side. Fold up the elastic a bit in the middle to ensure that the edges are stretched out where you pinned them. This is the point that needs attention at the moment.

D. Lay the other piece of the mask you created on the table. This second one should be laid on the first with the right side facing down.

E. Place your felt on top of the second mask piece you just laid on the first. Make sure that these pieces align well and that all the edges are in order. Pin all these layers together, but leave some space between the two pins so that you can know where you can avoid sewing when you get there. After doing this, turn the mask right side out.

F.  Remove all the pins that you used to hold the layers in place and starting from where you want the opening on your mask to be, start sewing these layer together. Use a 1/2 seam allowance to sew and go all the way around to the other part that is the left side of the openings you marked before you started sewing.

G.  Cut off the excesses from the stitch you just made. You want to make sure that the stitches are as clean as they should be and as such, you should trim all around the mask. While trimming, look out for the excess elastic and fabric. Get these out of the way so that you can proceed.

H.  Trimming will leave you with jagged edges. Turn these edges over themselves and get them to face inwards. Sew over what you have turned over.

I.  Turn the mask right side out by reaching into the small space you left when you were sewing the sides of the mask together. Start pulling the insides out

and do this slowly so that you do not tear what you
have created so far.

J.  When you are done turning the mask right side out,
    fold in any of the excess stitches carefully and make
    sure that all of them are tucked in well.

K.  After tucking in all edges of the mask, stitch it once
    again all-around. This time, you will be stitching
    closer to the top of the mask. This is called a top
    stitch and you should use a running stitch for it.

L.  After the last stitch, stretch the mask and make sure
    that there are no creases. You are done with your
    mask.

This is what the mask looks like upon completion

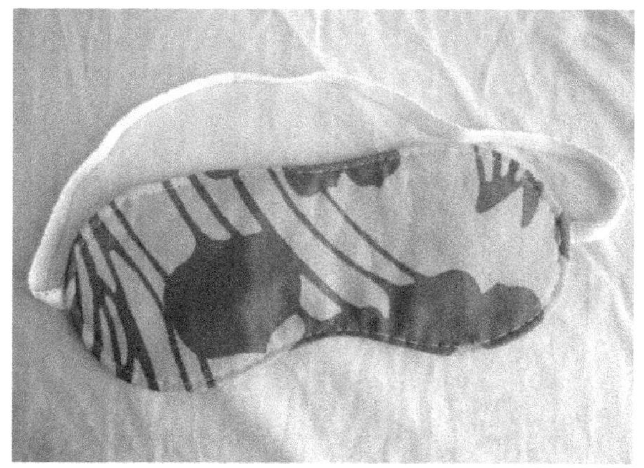

## Monogram Felt Pouch

This is a quick project you can embark upon at any time and complete within an hour or two. The best part of this is that you can customize this pouch at any time and create something different from what you already have. It is the perfect gift idea for a loved one, and because you can customize it, there are almost no limits to what you can create.

Here's how you go about it;

## Supplies you need

A. A felt piece (in the color of the pouch you want to create)

B.  DMC floss

C.  Fabric scrap of about 5" x 5"

D.  Scrap of fusible fleece.

E.  Zipper (about 7")

F.  Printed letter or shape.

## Directions

A.  Lay out your felt and make a line down the center. Make sure the line you are making is parallel to the shorter side of the felt material.

B.  Make a mark in the centre of the line you just drew. This will be for the zipper of the pouch. This line should measure about 11/4" from the end of the center line you drew at first.

C.  At the center of the line you drew in step one, cut out a tiny rectangle that will just be large enough to fit the pouch's zipper.

D.  Print the front letter or symbol unto the pouch. To do this

- Choose the letter you want to use and place it against the spread-out felt.
- Outline the letter on the pouch by printing it out on the felt with a chalk marker.

E. Now that you have the letter printed, snip into the outline and cut along the lines of the letter you printed on the felt.

F. Fuse the scrap of fabric you have and fuse it to a scrap of fusible fleece. Depending on the size of the letter you have printed, you will need a scrap piece big enough to cover it up.

G. Place the felt over the clothing scrap that has the fleece on it. Make sure that the fleece comfortably covers up the whole letter you cut out on the felt. From the front of the felt, do a running stitch to hold all the sides of the letter you printed on the felt in place.

H. Attach your zipper to the small rectangle you have in the middle of the felt fabric.

I. Fold the felt fabric in two with the backsides facing themselves. Attach these sides with a running stitch but this time, make sure that you make the stitches a bit tighter than they usually are. Before turning the pouch out again, do a blanket stitch all around the pouch. This will act as finishing to your pouch and ensures that you do not end up with rough and exposed edges.

You should have something like this

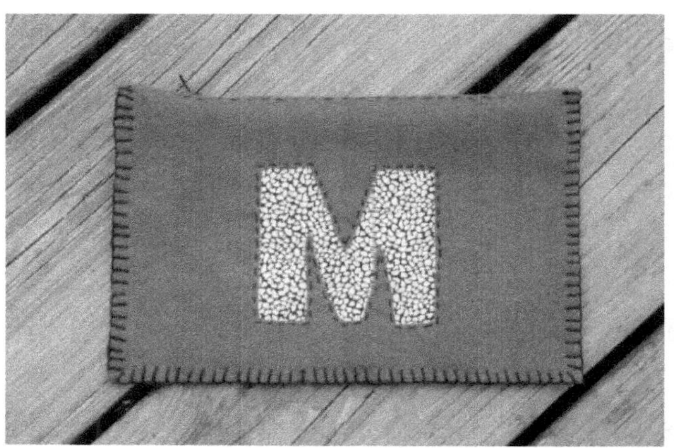

**Felt Christmas Tree**

This is one piece you should have in your house, especially as the season for Christmas begins to arrive. It is easy to make, does not require a lot of technical knowledge, not to mention that the trees turn out to be beautiful if you do a great job.

**Supplies you need**

A. Felting materials.
B. Beading needles and thread to match
C. Roving (green, red and other colors of the Christmas tree).
D. Beads; 4mm and 8mm assortment beads.

**Directions**

A. Collect enough roving that you will need to fashion the body of the tree. This should be enough for you to roll into the shape of a triangle.

B. Create another ball from the roving and attach this ball to the top of the roving. Make sure these two sides are not mismatched but are evenly connected to themselves. Begin poking the tree into shape with your needle. Pay the same attention to all sides of your tree as you work so that you do not lose the shape you are trying to preserve.

C. Create a flat bottom for the tree. Achieve this by poking the lower part of the tree inside and making sure that everything you are doing is even, as usual.

D. At the center of the top of your tree, create a hole with the tip of your needle and attach some of the free roving in this hole.

E. Attach the length of red roving at the tree's base and felt it into place with the needle. As you do this, pay close attention so that you tuck excess red felt under the tree.

F. Go ahead to decorate the tree with small ornaments and beads. This is what the Christmas tree looks like

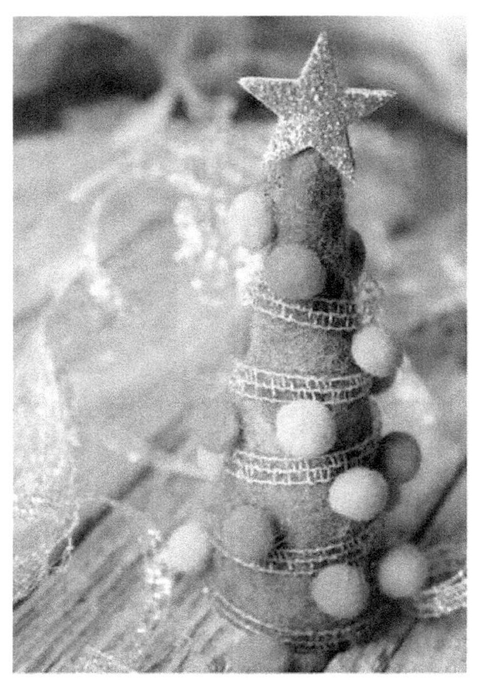

<h1 style="text-align:center;"><u>The end... almost!</u></h1>

Hey! We've made it to the final chapter of this book, and I hope you've enjoyed it so far.

If you have not done so yet, I would be incredibly thankful if you could take just a minute to leave a quick review on Amazon

Reviews are not easy to come by, and as an independent author with a little marketing budget, I rely on you, my readers, to leave a short review on Amazon.

Even if it is just a sentence or two!

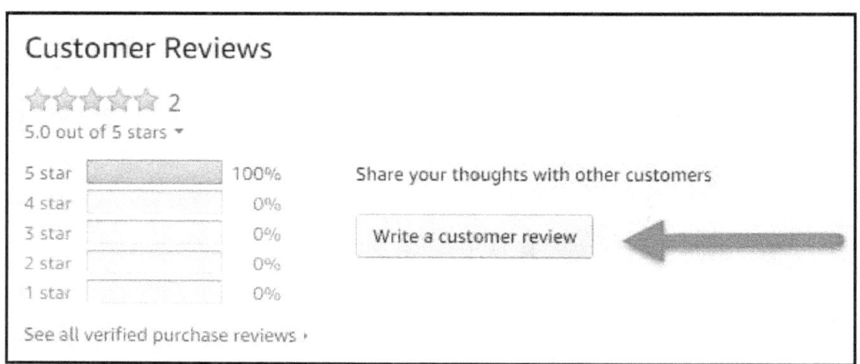


So if you really enjoyed this book, please...

>> Click here to leave a brief review on Amazon.

I truly appreciate your effort to leave your review, as it truly makes a huge difference.

# Chapter 6

## Needle Felting Frequently Asked Questions (FAQs)

Here are a few questions that have come up repeatedly as people hav practiced needle felting over time.

What tools do I need to get started with needle felting and where can I get these tools?

Answer; to get started with needle felting, you do not need a lot. All you need are felting needles, felting mat, wool, and time for the project at hand. Most of these items can be purchased online or in retail stores close to where you are.

1. What wool is most suitable for felting and where can I find it?

Answer; there is really not one answer to this. There are many types of wool out there for you to choose from, and all of these have their unique benefits and demerits. All you need to do is know the kind of wool that is needed for the project you have at hand and use it. You can look up the best wool for any project online, and find places where you can purchase them.

2. How do I make sure that my project comes out smoothly and without roughness?

Answer; creating smooth and beautiful projects is not something you can do in a day. It takes an amount of carefulness and constant practice to get this done. However, there are best practices that can help you here;

- Start with a firm base. If the project demands that you make use of something like a firm base, spend time creating this base and making sure that it is to the standard you are looking for.
- Felt properly. Felting can be a strenuous task and if you are not careful, there is every tendency that you may end up wanting to get it over with. However, one sure way to get the best results when you felt is by felting properly. Spread your efforts evenly across the project and see to it that you are not leaving a side unattended unless those were your intentions from the start.
- Use the right needles for the right projects. In an earlier part of this book, you were told about the

different sizes of needles and what you can use them for. Stick to this plan, so you do not end up with bad looking projects.

3.  Do felting needles wear out?

Answer; yes, they do. When used over time, or when not handled and stored as needed, felting needles wear out eventually. As a way around getting stuck, make sure that you have some felting needles with you as you prepare to embark upon any felting project.

4. What is the difference between wet felting and needle felting?

Answer; these two are all forms of felting and they are hinged on the same processes and theories; they use friction to transform loose wool fibers into a dense wool felt. However, the method through which this is achieved makes them different.

Wet felting draws upon the use of hot water, soap, and the subjection to use sheer force to cause the shrinking of the wool. On the other hand, needle felting achieves the same thing, but with the use of a special kind of needle.

5.  Can I combine wet and needle felting?

Answer; yes, you can. These two felting techniques are usually combined to join two distinct items, fix ornaments on designs, and so on. Projects that have been wet felted but have come out with dents can be salvaged (to an extent) using specific needle felting skills. However, it takes a lot of skill to combine these two techniques. If you must, please consult helpful content that teaches you how to get that done.

6.  Must I use wool for felting?

Answer; while wool is the most common material used for felting, it is not the only material used for felting. Any hair fiber from mammals can be used for the process and the results can be replicated in these hair fibers. Also, as long as the animal is a mammal, pet hair can be used for felting. However, it is vital that you know that the amount of hair you can get from smaller animals is only small and will limit the amount of work you will be able to achieve with it. If you are looking to get something little done, by all means, make use of the pet hair - if that's what works for you.

7.  Why did my felting project shrink?

Answer; shrinking is to be expected as you felt. As the fibers begin to lock in, and air is expelled from the wool, it will begin to reduce in size. However, if you notice a drastic and questionable decline in size, it could be as a result of the;

- The type of wool involved. Some wool types shrink by 20%, while others shrink by 40% or more. This, to a large extent, accounts for the decrease in the size of the wool as the project unfolds. If you are not sure how much your wool shrinks, try out the project with a little amount of wool (called a swatch) and watch what happens.

# Conclusion

Needle felting is an amazing way to let go of the creative juices flowing within you. When you learn the ropes of how needle felting is done, you will see that with just the right tools, patience, and the will to get better at it, you will surely get better at it.

This book has walked you through the process of becoming an intermediate needle felting craftsperson. From the place of not knowing how to navigate needle felting, you have been introduced to the concept, seen the tools that you need to get started, walked through a few easy projects you can embark upon and complete immediately, and you have also seen the answers to a few FAQs that could have kept you perplexed.

With the knowledge at your disposal, you should be able to get started with needle felting.

This is the best time to get started with needle felting. Put all you have seen and learned to use, and continuously grow from there.

Who knows? This may just be the next best craft for you to stick your teeth into.